THE SECOND SEX

MICHAEL ROBBINS

The SECOND SEX

PENGUIN POETS

PENGUIN BOOKS

Published by the Penguin Group
Penguin Group (USA) LLC
375 Hudson Street
New York, New York 10014

USA | Canada | UK | Ireland | Australia | New Zealand | India | South Africa | China
penguin.com
A Penguin Random House Company

First published in Penguin Books 2014

LIBRARY OF CONGRESS CATALOGING-IN-PUBLICATION DATA
Robbins, Michael, 1972–
[Poems. Selections]
The second sex / Michael Robbins.
pages cm.—(Penguin Poets)
ISBN 978-0-14-312664-5 (paperback)
I. Title.
PS3618.O315244A6 2014
811'.6—dc23
2014014466

Printed in the United States of America
1   3   5   7   9   10   8   6   4   2

Set in Adobe Garamond Pro with Trade Gothic and Pump
Designed by Ginger Legato

to the memory of Bill Knott

CONTENTS

Look at your money. No one is smiling.

—ALLAN PETERSON

THE SECOND SEX

Springtime in Chicago in November

Springtime in Chicago in November.
My forty-first year to heaven.
My left hand wants to know
what my right hand is doing.
Oh. Sorry I asked.

First comes love, which I disparage.
I blight with plagues a baby carriage.
Green means go and red means red.
Now we're cooking with Sudafed.

Steer by, deerfly. I hereby declare
the deer tick on my derriere
a heretic. Derelict, hunker down.
Get the Led out, Goodman Brown.

Get thee behind me, Nathan.
Horseman, ramble on.
Springtime snows white hairs on me.
Green means go and go means gone.

Live Rust

In the clearing I stand,
a boxer! Putting all your shit
in boxes, dragging the boxes
to this stupid clearing.

A man walks into his forties.
Says, *You lost me at "hello."*
I'm tying balloon animals.
Here you go. That's a rooster.

To burn out or to fade away?
I'm keeping my options open.
I'm looking for option C.
I'm boning up on Coptic.

I'm scrolling past the Dead Sea,
talking to Christ on the road
from Kiss My Ass to Damascus.
I kick my prick. I refute it THUS.

Be tawdry for me, thou.
Be like unto Sierra Mist
when it opens in the first
cold of spring. Be a Chippewa.

According to the oral history,
outside the Tastee Freez

you sucked on a chili dog
with your head between your knees.

The United States of Fuck You Too
is what you're about to receive.
You can shoot all the kids you like,
but you can never leave.

The mind is a terrible thing.
That outboard motor.
The tedium is the message.
The chimp signs *hugs* in his enclosure.

Is this Mick Jagger which I see before me?
Come, let me clutch thee.
I consider the lilies beneath me.
I tell the Magdalene not to touch me.

I tell the miniature schnauzer not to swarm.
I tell my willy it's getting warm.
I tell the content to fuck the form.

Sonnets to Edward Snowden

Who is the United States?
The grassy knoll elaborates.
Ask not what the Dew can do for you.
Ask about our special rates

for armed forces personnel.
All right, then, I'll go to hell.
These colors don't run—
red, white, and carbohydrate gel.

Navy SEALs are good to go
for *AvP* 2.0.
All along the White House fence

the Redskins mascot leads the chants.
Full fathom five Osama lies.
The blue-chip Dow industrials rise.

Who is the United States?
A snail paces by the Golden Gate's
anti-swan-dive hotline sign.
The snail is going to be fine.

Disabling a suicide
detector is prohibited.
A snail searches a starless sky
with the bionic arm he calls an eye.

The stars have got the bee disease.
The disappearing colonies
are no longer buzzworthy.

So ferry cross New Jersey.
I'm a black kid in a hoodie.
This land's the place I love. Et odi.

Who is the United States?
A grief ago—I'm bad with dates—
our fathers brought forth a queer
shoulder in a convex mirror.

I find it hard.
It was hard to found.
Unscrew the lids from the jars!
Prometheus outbound

on Aeroflot follows the Moskva
down to Gorky Park.
I'm proud to be a terrorist.

Mistakes were made at Plymouth Rock.
You might not be aware of this.
The ant's a centaur, more or less.

The Second Sex

After the first sex, there is no other.
I stick my gender in a blender
and click send. Voilà!
Your new ex-girlfriend.

You cuckold me with your husband.
I move a box with Ludacris.
The captain turns on, we begin our descent.
Be gentle with me, I'm new to this.

I say the wrong thing. I have OCD.
My obsessive compulsions are disorderly.
I say the wrong thing, did I already say?
I drive my dominatrix away.

The coyote drives her in a false-bottomed van.
He drops her in the desert. The bluffs are tan.
She'll get a job at Chili's picking up butts.
I feel ya, Ophelia, I say to my nuts.
And there is pansies. That's for thoughts.

That's Incredible!

I will pull an airplane with my teeth
and I will pull an airplane with my hair.
I write about cats. Cats, when you read this,
write about me. Be the change you want to see.

I've legally changed my name to Whites Only.
Changed it back, I should say.
DO NOT TRY THIS AT HOME made me
the man I am today.

That, and the University of Phoenix.
Old man, take a look at my life.
Charles Simic, in the gloaming, with a roach,
take a look at my life. I'm a lot like you.

A man stands up and says I will catch
a bullet in my teeth! *That's incredible!*
He eats a sword, hilt first, and spits
up a million people persons.

A dolphin pulls an airplane with its blowhole
and keeps the black box for itself.
Bottleneck dolphins don't even have bones,
yet here we are, giving them medals . . .

This is my ass. And that is a hole
in ground zero. I know which is which.
It's the one with the smoke pouring out.
This is my handle; this is my spout.

Be Myself

I took back the night. Wrested it
from the Chinese, many of whom
were shorter than me.
Two billion outstretched Chinese
hands, give or take a few
thousand amputees.

A cheap knockoff, the night
proved to be—*Nokla*
not *Nokia* on the touch screen.
Well, even Old Peng gotta eat,
Confucius say. Or maybe that
was Cassius Clay.

In me, folks, a movable object
meets a resistible force. I haven't
worked a day since the accident
of birth. Born of woman,
my father the same. Make love
then war. I'll bring round the car.

These children that I spit on
are immune to my consultations.
I'll have none myself. It isn't
(*Write* it!) a fiasco. I am small,
I contain platitudes.

Günter Glieben Glauchen Glöben

Says here to burn the rich and take their shit.
I'm paraphrasing. I'm barely grazing
the surplus. Do the rich have inner lives,
like little lambs and Antigone?
They never give me their money.

Bill Gates, the great humanitarian,
stands upon a peak in Darien.
I said Bill, I believe this is killing me.
A sculptor sees the statue in the slab,
the shiv in the toothbrush. The stab.

I plump for Red October. Sink or swim
or wade or creep or fly or soak
it all in kerosene. Miguel Hernández,
tell me, if you know, why there's a darkness

on the edge of credit. My student loans?
Forget it. Burn it up. Let's go for broke.
Watch the shares go up in smoke. Nostalgia's
just another word that starts with *No*.

Seasons in the Abyss

Du Fu, you dufus, that's not
a goose. You're drunk.
Please allow me to introduce . . .
no, that's not your horse.
(No, nor woman neither.)

Into every life a little
Freud must fall. I'm a fraud.
I stole that pun. Like I said:
I'm afraid. Into every light
a little moth must blunder . . .

Cue power ballad.
I don't know what to call a spade.
The sky will lately swish stuff.
I open my barbaric yap.
Du Fu joins me on the veranda.

We are old and full of crap.
The millionaires across the way,
their homes are all ablaze.
We like it when those homes collapse
like moths before clichés.

To Anthony Madrid

Distant is our exit, unmoving the traffic;
useful are the implements of a trade;
movies in 3-D are intolerable.

Ash on the wind, nobody's naming names;
neither the drive-thru voice that takes my order
nor the divine can be clearly understood.

Bleak is the arbor, pungent the homeless;
apples for apples, a fool's swap;
never write down your password.

Left lane closed, stonecraft asks patience;
an athlete's shoe, many covet it;
the wise are full of loathing.

Tick harbors pathogens, bull's-eye rash;
who trusts will be deceived;
one in five goes undiagnosed.

Summer in the city, girl out of college
cannot install the A/C;
three dollars to withdraw cash.

Long the line for coffee, great my need;
the shaven adepts seat their gods in grain;
no right turn on red.

North wind, trees bow down;
gaily skitters the Juicy Juice carton;
a car alarm is no sign of theft.

Fresh out the kitchen is the remix,
strong the noise of the ambulance bay;
pull out slow until you can see.

Buttered and shaggy the bees;
a man fishes in a dumpster,
I look away; angels are real.

Longtime listener, first-time caller;
dogs know more than they let on;
show me on the doll where I touched you.

The cleric bars the clinic doors;
single-celled, the House Majority Whip;
very well then, I contradict you.

Distant our exit, unmoving the traffic;
useless the smoking cessation kit;
a wise adage, Expect Delays.

Not Fade Away

Half of the Beatles have fallen
and half are yet to fall.
Keith Moon has set. Hank Williams
hasn't answered yet.

Children sing for Alex Chilton.
Whitney Houston's left the Hilton.
Hendrix, Guru, Bonham, Janis.
They have a tendency to vanish.

Bolan, Bell, and Boon by car.
How I wonder where they are.
Hell is now Jeff Hanneman's.
Adam Yauch and three Ramones.

[This space held in reserve
for Zimmerman and Osterberg,
for Bruce and Neil and Keith,
that sere and yellow leaf.]

Johnny Cash and Waylon Jennings,
Stinson, Sterling, Otis Redding.
Johnny Thunders and Joe Strummer,
Ronnie Dio, Donna Summer.

Randy Rhoads and Kurt Cobain,
Patsy Cline and Ronnie Lane.
Poly Styrene, Teena Marie.
Timor mortis conturbat me.

Out of the Cellar

Windows to wash and dust to dust.
You must improve your archaic bust.
In the name of extremes, and of
Krispy Kremes, and of mascara metal,
amen. I mean, come on,

I've known rivers. I know seems.
I rent my shoes. Daddy worked
the pneumatic tubes. Hold steady,
Holy See. You've really got
a hold on me.

Because your friends don't dance,
I'm applying for grants. Thanks,
Guildenstern and gentle Rosencrantz.
I don my customary suit of solemn black.
It takes a nation of morons to hold me back.

Peel Off the Scabs

Peel off the scabs! Unscrew
the daughters themselves from their jambs!
God became a man,
surely I can do the same.

I don't know wrong from light.
I can't tell my bright from left.
I really must be going.
I must be going soft.

I and I am I because I know
I wanna be your little dog.
Don't spit me out. Just swallow me.
I'll be your burning synagogue.

O Captain! my Tennille! the Eagles
will come and pull out his eyes.
Jesus coming back, they say,
and we'll all shout *Surprise!*

Is it any wonder I've got
too much blood on my hands? The calls
are coming from inside the house.
I'm sick of my insane demands.

Mississippi

Old news, Orion, old Ford:
come in, mockingbird.

Old saw, old gong, old giant:
come in like a lion.

Old tree, old ship, old song:
go along to get along.

Old blues, blue blood, blood orange:
how much is the damage.

New house, free range, thin herd:
hear a discouraging word.

New moon, full dark, seaweed:
at first you don't succeed.

Slow god, Gilead, old gate:
come to those who wait.

Old snow, old street, old fence:
rooms to let fifty cents.

Late night, last chance, light load:
get on down the road.

Sunday Morning

Must you flush the toilet
while I'm in the shower?
That's a metaphor. It means:
one system, contrary aims.

Let us say that I have come
from beyond the Lyme fields
and ironworks of mortal men.
Would you flush the toilet then?

It's a yes or no question.
Sometimes I think you're in a coma
for there is no pupillary response
when I shine a penlight in your eyes.

Still speaking metaphorically.
We're all adults here,
except for the children.
We all have someplace we'd rather be.

Once, not many winters ago,
a man could record his favorite show
on magnetic tape in plastic casing
and enjoy it at his leisure.

Or so I imagine it,
living alone with the cat,

my amanuensis and all that.
Visitors tell her that she's fat.

Anthony comes around to play
"Burning Airlines Give You So Much More"
on my brand-new Yamaha.
I read him what I wrote that day.

I step from the capsule
out onto the surface of my apartment.
From here the earth looks like the set
of the Verizon Halftime Report.

I make the beast with no backs.
Someday a real rain will come
and wash all the scum
off my sheets.

I support the unborn child's right
to be spared the ghastly sight
of this brightly burning world,
this swiftly tilting dumpster.

All new speedways boogie
and misty mountains hop.
The telephone's been cut off,
I'm waiting for the clocks to stop.

If you love something, set it free—
that's stupid. Keep it close.
If I've killed one man,
I've killed most.

I'm having a feelings attack
out of the blue. Into the black
site, the multisided mudslide.
I'm just trying to find the bridge.

I Skype with Rose.
The heart knows what it knows.
Rose says, "Go put a shirt on."
All my friends are Scorpios.

I live alone with the cat.
It's been a long time.
Been a long lonely
lonely lonely lonely lonely time.

40th Anniversary Edition

It's the Chinese Year of the Fire Drill.
I walk the fields—alfalfa, falafel, falderal.
Nothing out here but syllables, high as
Aegean okra, and a few post-agrarian silos,
dotless i's that dormice catch some z's in.
They're rich like me, this time of the season.

Convair CV-300, play that dead band's
last black-box seconds. I can't imagine that Can's
records were favorites of Ronnie Van Zant's.
Gary Rossington (later he married Dale Krantz)
broke both arms and legs and, yep, his pelvis,
two months after, yup, the death of Elvis.

Star Wars had opened in Wichita, Kansas.
I don't think anyone knew who Can was.
I listened to Kiss and Shaun Cassidy.
But when Skynyrd's bird dropped out of the sky
(I'll spare you the pun I've prepared on "free")
we sang *Watergate does not bother me.*

Turn those speakers up full blast, and all that.
Nel mezzo nevermind—*pace* Foghat—
what a loose ride, what a fast ride too.
Remaster *Tago Mago*, add bonus tracks, reissue.

Overnight

The FedEx logo, feral,
felling deer with its arrow,
likes shooting monkeys
in a barrel. It gets Lyme disease.

The ironies! Arrows and
the telltale Target logo rash
I sing. The love of evil.
The root of cash.

My bluish and my human foot
around the child soldier's neck
absolutely has to be there.
We demur to dissect.

I shall be telling this far hence
in a speeding Mystery Van
traveling furiously toward you.
Get out as early as you can.

Within a Budding Grove

The rabies virus is half my age.
Its engine's any bartender.
It's part meerkats at the zoo at prayer,
part Nobodaddy Tabernacle Choir.

All boners are my brothers.
Alps on Alps arise.
The waitress serves the fatal virus.
She's never seen *The Rockford Files.*

O huntress, suitably attired,
you're going to need a tetanus shot.
You've got a suitable vagina.
I do not want what you haven't got.

I come from a land of ice and snow.
I'll reboot your Southern charms
with the brute brute boot of a brute like me.
All boners are my brothers in arms.

Poem Beginning with a Line from
Samuel Johnson

Clear your mind of cunt.
I can't.
I put on my pants
one day at a time.

I have an eight-track mind.
It shoots ink to confuse.
I support
its right to choose.

When I was a child
I caught a fleeting glimpse
of two balloons.
Just a little pinprick.

I'm a certain snatch of light
passing through
a double slit.
If observed, I behave

like a prodigal,
not a wave.
I'm neither both
nor and.

You'll never understand.
You'll never undersea.
I feel like a natural woman
is just too real for me.

In the Air Tonight

All my love come tumbling down
and I get wild pregnant with Jesus.
I feel a wild harbor in my pants
and the boats with all their lights.

I have some oats in a thing of leather.
My toast always lands Christ-side up.
Kid! It's coming out my *ears*.
Don't you want to be there when we all get born?

Let's carry rope together in a glade.
Boom Boom Mancini survived on ferns
and roots for a month on Fire Island.
I led the search party. It's what I do.

I too dislike you. I rock down to
Electric Avenue. Let's reinvent then die
behind the wheel. I've been waiting
for this moment for all my life.
Oh Lord.

Friend of the Devil

See here on the ultrasound,
that thing that looks like a comma?
It will separate the elements
in a series. I can't believe we're even
having this conversation to begin with.

The womb's a fine and private place,
or am I thinking of a doughnut?
You ask me, the hippies still have
a lot to answer for. But no one
ever asks me. I smell pasta.

I was a nurse during the war.
The soldiers in their dying pleaded,
"Can you get one of the other nurses?"
I know what no duck knows.
Tomorrow is Thursday.

Come, Lord Jesus,
let us not bandy words.
I too have followed the Dead.
I saw you and the devil talking.
Tell me, bluntly, what he said.
Weren't you just a little tempted?

Rhymes

I went down to Nag Hammadi.
What's your name and who's your daddy.

Hamper's full, the laundry's dry.
These pots might have some jinn inside.

That whale must answer for his crimes.
He ate four trainers and some lions.

Devil horns and nothing else on.
Matthew Murdock, Foggy Nelson.

Foggy notion just crossed my mind.
Trouble ahead, lotion behind.

Get with the program, mandrake root.
Let raven croak and howlet hoot.

A liver, observe, is eating an eagle.
The liver is me, we learn in the sequel.

Sometimes an eagle is just a cigar.
Mock on, mock on, Truffaut, Godard.

A bout of sniffles, something's off.
Turn your head to the side and cough.

Daughters and sons, dollars and cents.
Cat's in the cradle, dog far hence.

About that soufflé, a word if I may.
Roadside abortion, curds and whey.

If it's romance you're after in Phoenix,
just ask a teen girl for a kleenex.

Could you finish up a little faster?
You're old enough to be my sister.

My battle cry is Nevermore.
I give these suckerfish what for.

I ruin them. I'm through with men.
I build the new Jerusalem.

This earth, my sole inheritance,
spits up its precious lubricants.

I kick an empty gas can.
Behold: the next-to-last man.

The Song Remains the Same

Comfortably platinum,
they bang a gong, the old masters.
Jägermeister underwrites
their Stratocasters.

My childhood's reunited
and it feels so good. It feels
like making love for money should.
Money changes chicks for free.
It changes Freddie Mercury.

Ave Regina!
How high that highest Bic
lights the arena.

What is the use of rocking,
and there is no end of rocking.
AOR's blocked aortas clog
Friday Night Rock Block,
but Zoso what, black dog?
It's half-past past is prologue.

Sweat, Piss, Jizz & Blood

The great nation of California
shuts out the lights, one by one.
I'm next door in the saguaro.
I must expel the Mexican.

Warren Zevon, Levon Helm
slip into a slippery elm—
fall, gash, crash that gold-
vermillion dollar bash.

Mississippi trinity:
fetus, flag, and F-150.
The bee, a tiny mason, is
expert in fruition.
The honey-drip, the bee-loud buzz
of Jimmy Page's Gibson.

You say that this is all there is:
sweat and piss and blood and jizz.
But I'm from wheat and dust and flat,
and I was born to marvel at
the Jayhawks in 2008.
I don't believe you: God is great.

Country Music

God bless the midnight bus depot,
the busted guitar case.
God bless diazepam,
its dilatory grace.

God keep Carl Perkins warm
and Jesus Christ erase
my name from all the files in
the county's database.

The dog that bit my leg
the night I left the state,
Lord won't you let
his vaccines be up to date.

West Point to the south of me,
Memphis to the north.
In between is planted with
pinwheels for the Fourth.

Smokestack Lightning, Jesus Christ—
whatever your name is—
bless my fingers on these strings,
I'll make us both famous.

How about that, the new moon,
same as it ever was.

You must've been high as a kite
when you created us.

So hurry, hurry, step right up,
there's something you should see.
The sun shines on the bus depot
like a coat of Creole pink.

God keep the world this clean and bright
and easy to believe in
and let me catch my bus all right,
and then we'll call it even.

Oh Wow

The only reason you're not going to hell is you're already in it.
The *Fear Factor* contestant says he's in it to win it.
Science, the opiate of the elite, asks too many questions.
I become tired and sick, till I wander off by myself and listen in
    perfect silence to *The Sun Sessions*.
Why is there something rather than something else is a question
    only Southern rock can answer.
The cattle all have brucellosis. Grandma's dead of cancer.

The astronauts of my youth plant the flashing MTV logo on
    the moon.
I thought of that historic moment on the day Steve Jobs was taken
    from us too soon.
The artist formerly known as Sting gives back rubs to the war orphans;
Swami Svatmarama distributes copies of the *Hatha Yoga* to boost
    the orphans' endorphins.
Would you care to make a small donation?
The orphans with remaining limbs give the dharma a standing
    ovation.

Oh wow, a guy came on your face and you wrote about it? That's
    so daring.
Let me be among the very first to say thanks for sharing.
If you need a writing tutor, I am programmed to oblige.
Lesson one: metaphor, a kind of bridge.
A blackbird can be looked at in a number of ways, including two.
A man and a woman are the loneliest number that you'll ever do.

On Making Mixes for Girls Who Won't Give
Death Metal a Chance

My reptile brain sheds its skin.
On its belly it goes supernova.
It got over getting over
that assimilated Jew, Jehovah.

My reptile brain chops off its tail
to watch it grow right back.
The family requests an autopsy.
My brain drops horribly in a pail.

Like a bulwark
breached for the very first time,
dear brain, once more unto!
There's someone bleeding all over you.

Down on all fours, brain.
Brain take a face full of quills.
You're still in love with dark
Satanic Hayley Mills.

In olden days a glimpse of stocking
would give me a lobotomy.
The very thought of me!
Out of the car, long hair, endlessly rocking.
Reptile brains are wasted on the young.

Butcher Holler

Got an empty shoe box for Xmas.
Every Xmas, same shoe box.
The theater of my dreams
I called it, for I dreamed of shoes.

Its realistic cardboard walls
enclosed a horseless expanse—
no lariat, no corral, no okay. So I
stole six U.S. Army mules,

named 'em Cattle Drive,
Train Job, Bank Job, Blow,
Adios Muchachos, and All
Deserts Have Cacti.

In fact, I also stole
their sires and dams.
A man should have a best-laid plan,
or what's a town dump for?

So mothers, tell your children
I'll need to see some ID.
Work on your looks, ye mighty.

Someday I'll have more shoes
than I know what to do.
Barefoot servants too.

Lose Myself

Yeah, I got the bug. Got razzle dazzle,
dazed and refused. I'm with stupid.
Step up, chump. I'm OK, cupid.
Main man on the data dump.

I'm erotic baggage and cholo spit.
I'm the motherfucking *the*.
I *invented* it. I'm a bucket
of Colonel Sanders,
Kentucky Fried Panzer man.

I'm a bare midriff in a sharkskin suit.
I got twenty-seven dollars!
I'm homing in on your boo.
It's all over now, Bobbie Sue.

Yet tarry awhile. Set a spell,
Big Bad Leroy Iffucan.
It takes three miracles to make a saint,
just one mistake to make a man.

Michael Jackson

Michael Jackson you gave us all and now you're nothing.
Michael Jackson one zillion dollars June 25, 2009.

I don't care if you lightened your skin.
I don't care if a pig in a poke
get out of a poke
and can't get back in.

For a while here an unusual man?
I'll say. The grave is gone and gray
as Gary. Mills shoulder dirty snow.
Let my people go.

Michael's mind out-Heroded stuff.
He lay with many a kid. I don't know
and you shouldn't act
like you know what he did.

And if they say *why, why,*
tell 'em that it's human nature.
Some men is an island.
The lighted sidewalk squares fall silent.

Political Poem for Michael Robbins to Sing

I am my twin brother Matthew Robbins.
I know how to light up a room.
I kill one bird with several stones.
Israeli jets light up Khartoum.

A savage servility slides
by on the way we are feeling
from Kabbalah to Kabul,
Daodejing to Darjeeling,

Shiite to Shinola,
Ob-La-Di to *objet* (a),
Ram a Lam to Ding Dong,
Obi-Wan to Ob-La-Da,

from Hopi to IHOP
and Mayan to Ramayana,
Robespierre to RoboCop,
yippee-ki-yay to kumbayah.

A savage serves me a slider.
Grease is the word for his face.
Michael Robbins, cute as a button.
My alibi, my donkey, my master race!

Twentieth Century Fox

Turns out I never made a lampshade
from, Jew or gentile, human skin.
I mean the Nazis didn't. Sometimes
I feel so evil, I get us confused.
Colonel Klink on his way to masseuse.

God is a spider, the moon's made of barf.
Wait—how did *I* get so smart?
Reading Foxe's *Martyrs*, its famous quote:
"Be of good comfort, Naomi Wolf."

Covering the election from the Persian Gulf,
it's Harold Bloom. I am the canon, hear me roar.
In the name of *Bush v. Gore*,
I plant my fat on the land.
I am woman. You wouldn't understand.

To the Drone Vaguely Realizing Eastward

This is a poem for President Drone.
It was written by a camel.
Can I borrow your phone?
This is for President Mark Hamill.

Newtown sounds a red alert.
Mark Hamill asks if Ernie's burnt.
Every camel's a first-person shooter.
The Prez's fez is haute couture.

It seems strange that he should be offended.
The same orders are given by him.
Paging Pakistan and Yemen.
Calling all the drone-dead children.

The camel can't come to the phone.
This is for the drone-in-chief.
Mumbai used to be Bombay.
The bomb bay opens with a queef.

Sweet Virginia

I got a letter from the government.
It said let there be night.
I went through your trash.
There was night, all right.
I consider how your light is spent.

I have butterflies a little bit.
I have some pills I take for it.
I've been up since four the day before.
Agony's a cinch to sham.

Don't worry about the environment.
Let it kill us if it can.
I give a tiny tinker's damn.
I put the ox behind the cart.
Consume away my snowblind heart.

Fastened to a service animal
it is waiting for the beep.
It is waiting for the right to change.
Hello, I know you're there, pick up.

Sticky Fingers

I practice Velcro mind,
tar baby mind. I stick
to my guns. I'm a major find.
Stick to my loo, my darling.
Stick to your own kind.

Stately, plump Wayne Manor!
Mattel, Adele, Adorno—
O DeLorean
on extended wings!

I know a guy who knows a guy.
The octopus of glam rock
shoplifting Tide. Ed Dorn,
Isadora Duncan, defend us!
Yes, Virginia, there is a.

Captain Kitty Pryde
of the *Exxon Valdez*,
sorry I missed your call. The wall
I pass through passes through
me and out the other side.

Big Country

Fiddle no further, Führer. Rome is built.
It took all day. Now let us so
love the world. I'm just thinking out loud.
My stigmata bring out my eyes.

The smallpox uses every part of the blanket,
and the forest is a lady's purse.
The Indian is a pink Chihuahua peeking
his head from the designer zipper.

Out here it's mostly light from the fifteenth
century slamming into the planet.
I can't see the forest for the burn unit.
All the planet does is bitch bitch bitch.

I know it's last minute but could you put
out my eyes? At the subatomic level,
helmeted gods help themselves to gold.
Up here? The body's an isolation ward.

Out Here in the Fields

Out here in the fields
a technician dims the light.
Too soon to say for sure
if this coheres all right.

You ask what time the elephant
sat upon the fence.
Sounds to me like time to get
a few new elephants.

I dress up like a razor blade
and hide inside an orange.
Petition, little children, one
who finds you less annoying.

No orange can be compelled
to self-incriminate.
The jury will disregard
the thirty-seventh state.

Longshoremen and long shores,
short piers and ships in port.
Third planet from the sun, I'm told.
It won't stand up in court.

You got moxie, kid, mixing
ricin in the suburbs.

I'm gonna be a nicer person
and emulate the lovebirds

with night-lights in their hips
and UC Davis eyes.
We'll sing the *Mary Hartman* theme
until the great assize.

Anna Wintour's discontented.
I'm bathing in the nude.
I'm erring on the side.
I'm pretty sure we're screwed.

This is rocket science
in the Desert Father style.
Those weirdos in their caves—
man, you should read their file.

They made war upon their privates.
They had insects in their beards.
Once you got 'em talking,
they'd prattle on for years.

And I'd be more like them
if I were less like this,
a billion points of glitter
in a fathomless abyss.

ACKNOWLEDGMENTS AND NOTES

Some of these ditties first appeared in *Commonweal*, *The Economy*, *The Hat*, *Hazlitt*, *Lemon Hound*, *Los Angeles Review of Books*, *Mississippi Review*, *The New Yorker*, *Poetry*, *Prelude*, and *The Walrus*. One love to the editors.

Overnight shipping thanks: Paul Slovak, Anthony Madrid, Steven Critelli.

Priority shipping thanks: Paige Ackerson-Kiely, Robert Archambeau, Zach Baron, Paul-Jon Benson, Mark Z. Danielewski (RIP Carl), Mark Fletcher, Virginia Heffernan, Ilya Kaminsky, Anahid Nersessian, Christa Robbins, Rose Schapiro, Dana Snitzky, Amber Tamblyn, Jen Vafidis.

"To the Drone Vaguely Realizing Eastward": See my essay "A Poem for President Drone" in *Los Angeles Review of Books* at http://lareviewofbooks.org/essay/a-poem-for-president-drone.

Photo: Clayton Hauck

Michael Robbins was born in Kansas during the Nixon administration. Sometime later, he received his PhD in English from the University of Chicago. His poetry and criticism have appeared in *The New Yorker, Poetry, Harper's,* and many other publications. He lives in America with the best cat in the world.

JOHN ASHBERY
Selected Poems
Self-Portrait in a Convex Mirror

TED BERRIGAN
The Sonnets

LAUREN BERRY
The Lifting Dress

JOE BONOMO
Installations

PHILIP BOOTH
Lifelines: Selected Poems,
1950–1999
Selves

JULIANNE BUCHSBAUM
The Apothecary's Heir

JIM CARROLL
Fear of Dreaming:
The Selected Poems
Living at the Movies
Void of Course

ALISON HAWTHORNE DEMING
Genius Loci
Rope

CARL DENNIS
Another Reason
Callings
New and Selected Poems
1974–2004
Practical Gods
Ranking the Wishes
Unknown Friends

DIANE DI PRIMA
Loba

STUART DISCHELL
Backwards Days
Dig Safe

STEPHEN DOBYNS
Velocities: New and Selected
Poems, 1966–1992

EDWARD DORN
Way More West: New and
Selected Poems

ROGER FANNING
The Middle Ages

ADAM FOULDS
The Broken Word

CARRIE FOUNTAIN
Burn Lake
Instant Winner

AMY GERSTLER
Crown of Weeds: Poems
Dearest Creature
Ghost Girl
Medicine
Nerve Storm

EUGENE GLORIA
Drivers at the Short-Time Motel
Hoodlum Birds
My Favorite Warlord

DEBORA GREGER
By Herself
Desert Fathers, Uranium
Daughters
God
Men, Women, and Ghosts
Western Art

TERRANCE HAYES
Hip Logic
Lighthead
Wind in a Box

NATHAN HOKS
The Narrow Circle

ROBERT HUNTER
Sentinel and Other Poems

MARY KARR
Viper Rum

WILLIAM KECKLER
Sanskrit of the Body

JACK KEROUAC
Book of Sketches
Book of Blues
Book of Haikus

JOANNA KLINK
Circadian
Raptus

JOANNE KYGER
As Ever: Selected Poems

ANN LAUTERBACH
Hum
If in Time: Selected Poems,
1975–2000
On a Stair
Or to Begin Again
Under the Sign

CORINNE LEE
PYX

PHILLIS LEVIN
May Day
Mercury

PATRICIA LOCKWOOD
Motherland Fatherland
Homelandsexuals

WILLIAM LOGAN
Macbeth in Venice
Madame X
Strange Flesh
The Whispering Gallery

ADRIAN MATEJKA
The Big Smoke
Mixology

MICHAEL MCCLURE
Huge Dreams: San Francisco
and Beat Poems

ROSE MCLARNEY
Its Day Being Gone

DAVID MELTZER
David's Copy: The Selected
Poems of David Meltzer

ROBERT MORGAN
Terroir

CAROL MUSKE-DUKES
An Octave Above Thunder
Red Trousseau
Twin Cities

ALICE NOTLEY
Culture of One
The Descent of Alette
Disobedience
In the Pines
Mysteries of Small Houses

WILLIE PERDOMO
The Essential Hits of
Shorty Bon Bon

LAWRENCE RAAB
The History of Forgetting
Visible Signs: New and Selected
Poems

BARBARA RAS
The Last Skin
One Hidden Stuff

MICHAEL ROBBINS
Alien vs. Predator
The Second Sex

PATTIANN ROGERS
Generations
Holy Heathen Rhapsody
Wayfare

WILLIAM STOBB
Absentia
Nervous Systems

TRYFON TOLIDES
An Almost Pure Empty Walking

ANNE WALDMAN
Gossamurmur
Kill or Cure
Manatee/Humanity
Structure of the World
Compared to a Bubble

JAMES WELCH
Riding the Earthboy 40

PHILIP WHALEN
Overtime: Selected Poems

ROBERT WRIGLEY
Anatomy of Melancholy and
Other Poems
Beautiful Country
Earthly Meditations: New and
Selected Poems
Lives of the Animals
Reign of Snakes

MARK YAKICH
The Importance of Peeling
Potatoes in Ukraine
Unrelated Individuals Forming
a Group Waiting to Cross